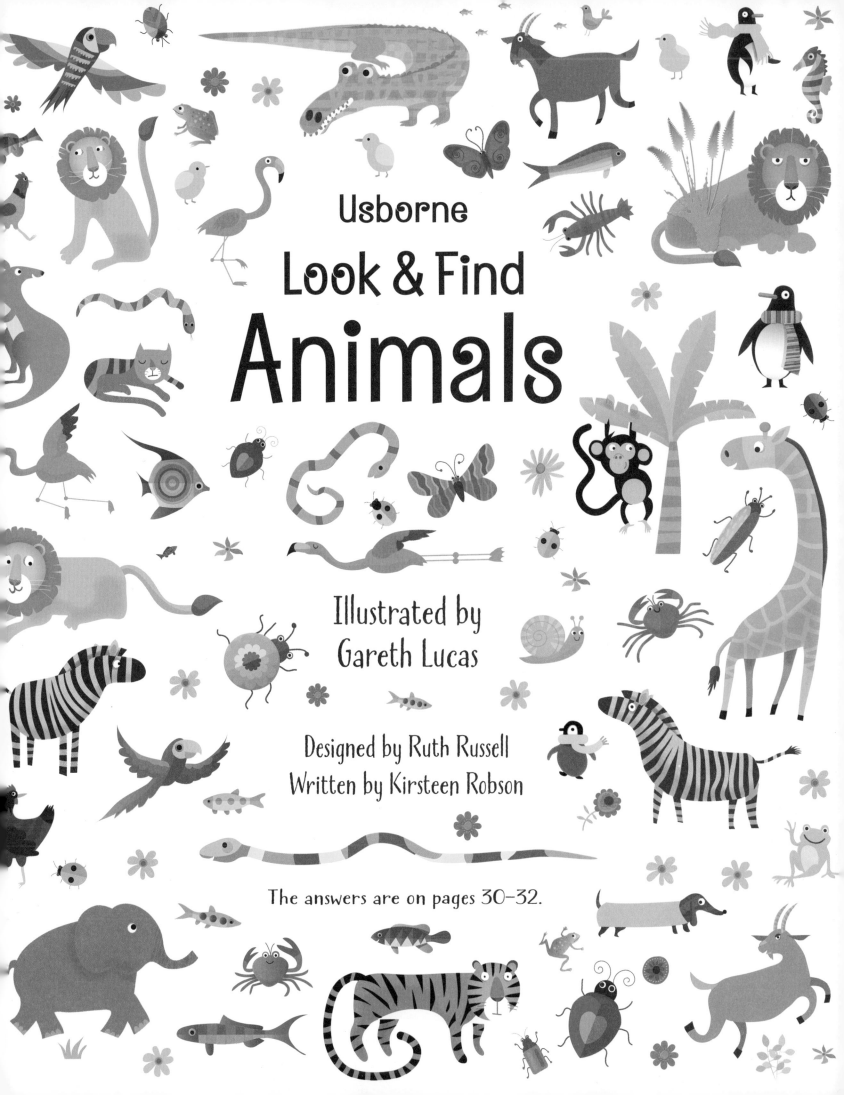

Usborne
Look & Find
Animals

Illustrated by
Gareth Lucas

Designed by Ruth Russell
Written by Kirsteen Robson

The answers are on pages 30–32.

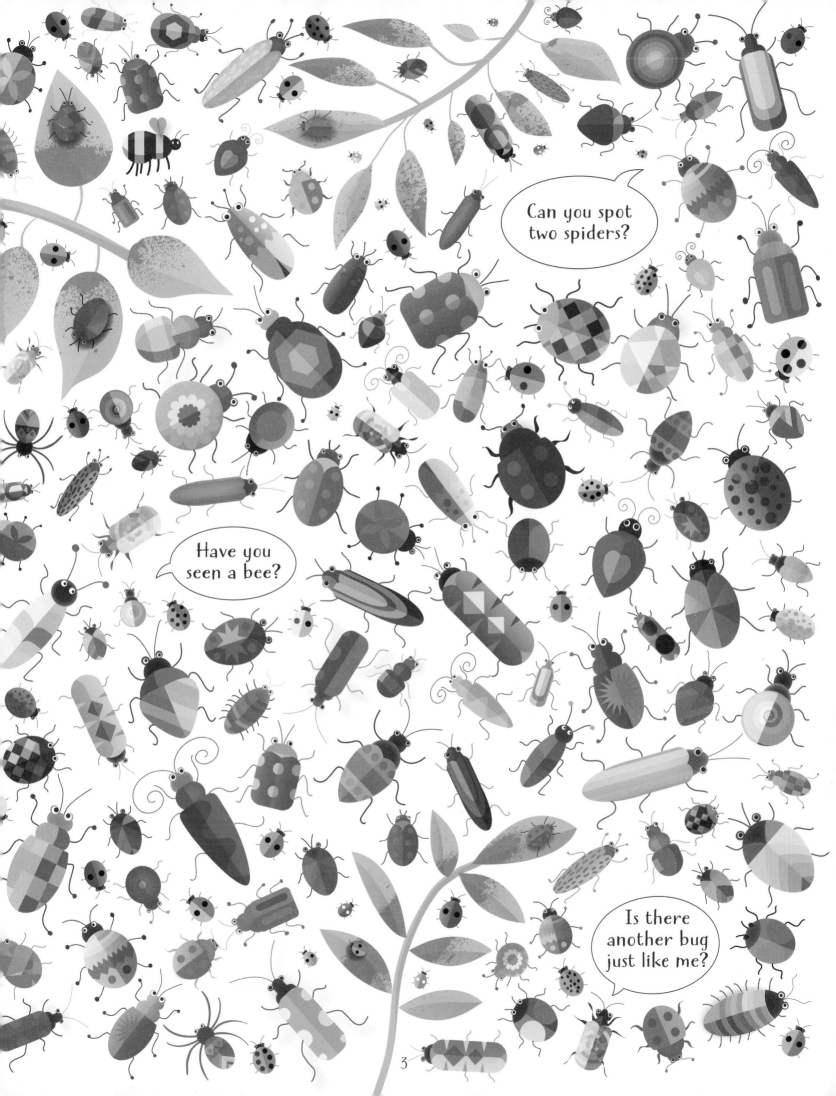

7

9

Where is the mouse?

Find two friends enjoying a water fight.

11

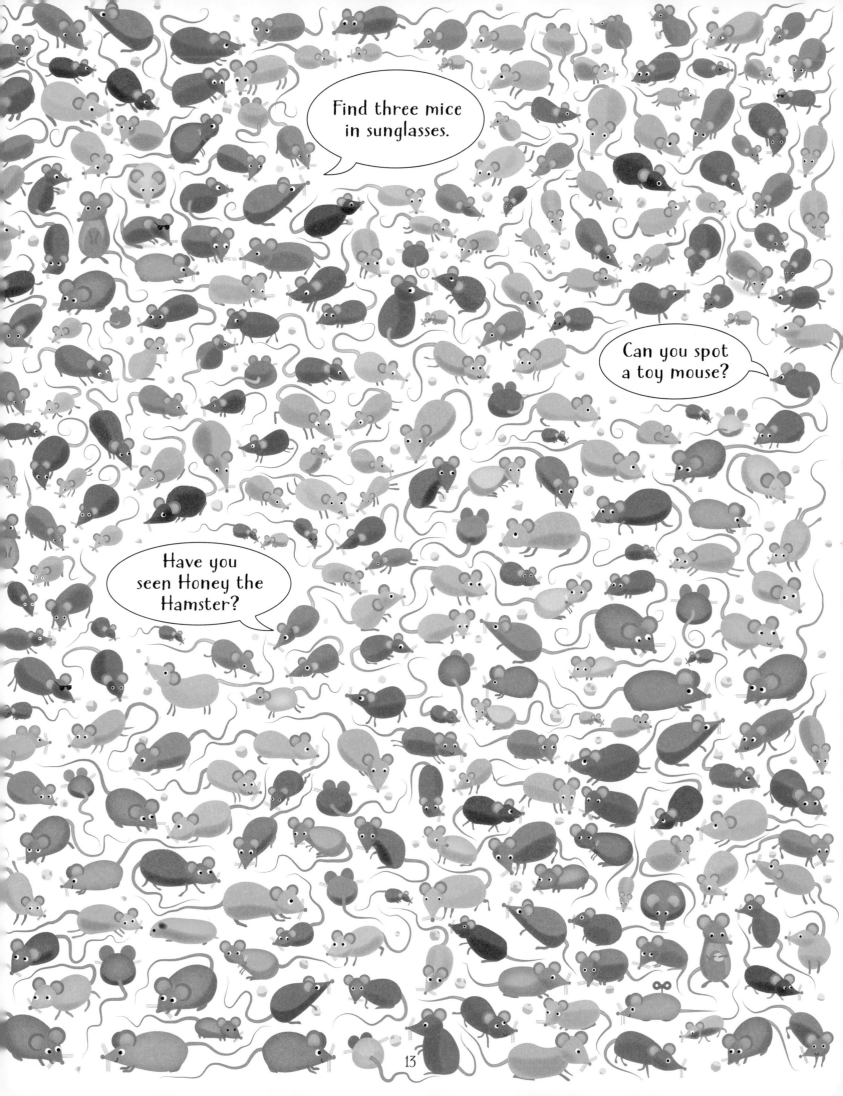

17

19

22

23

24

ANSWERS

The tiger is on page 1.

Cover

1

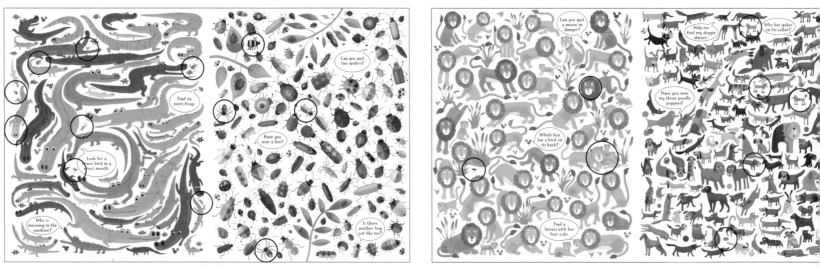

2-3

4-5

6-7

8-9

10–11

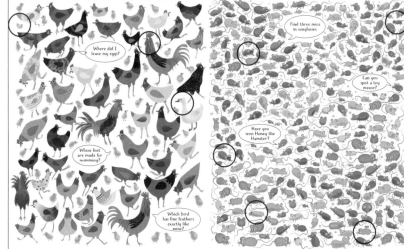

12–13

14–15

16–17

18–19

20–21

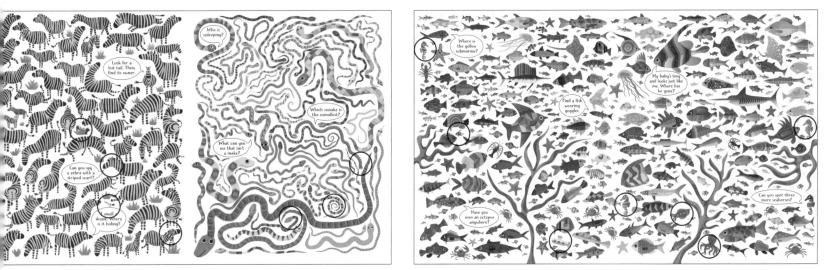

ANSWERS (continued)

There are 4 snails.

22–23

24–25

26–27

There are 6 butterflies.

28–29

This edition first published in 2018 by Usborne Publishing Ltd, Usborne House, 83–85 Saffron Hill, London, EC1N 8RT, England. www.usborne.com
Copyright © 2018, 2014 Usborne Publishing Ltd. The name Usborne and the devices 🏆 👂 are Trade Marks of Usborne Publishing Ltd. All rights reserved.
No part of this publication may be reproduced, stored in a retrieval system, or transmitted in any form or by any means, electronic, mechanical,
photocopying, recording or otherwise, without the prior permission of the publisher. UE. Printed in China.